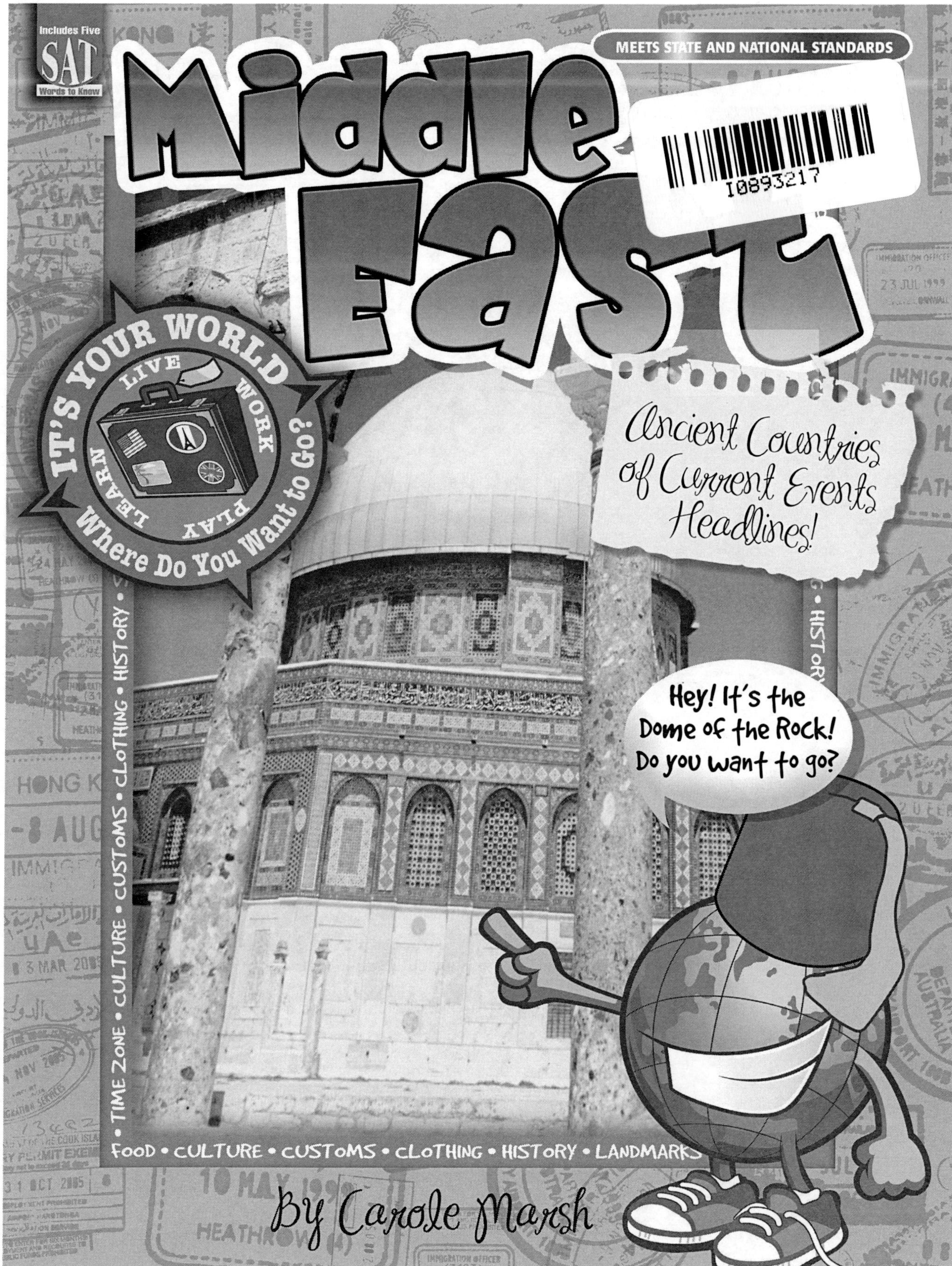
Includes Five
SAT
Words to Know
MEETS STATE AND NATIONAL STANDARDS
Middle East
IT'S YOUR WORLD
LIVE
WORK
PLAY
LEARN
Where Do You Want to Go?
Ancient Countries of Current Events Headlines!
Hey! It's the Dome of the Rock! Do you want to go?
TIME ZONE • CULTURE • CUSTOMS • CLOTHING • HISTORY
FOOD • CULTURE • CUSTOMS • CLOTHING • HISTORY • LANDMARKS
By Carole Marsh

Live • Work • Play • Learn

GALLOPADE INTERNATIONAL

Gallopade International is introducing SAT words that kids need to know in our books. The SAT words in this book have a gray box around them. Students can look up the definitions and increase their vocabulary. Happy Learning!

Gallopade is proud to be a member and supporter of these educational organizations and associations:

Association for the Study of African American Life and History
National Alliance of Black School Educators
American Booksellers Association
American Library Association
International Reading Association
National Association for Gifted Children
The National School Supply and Equipment Association
The National Council for the Social Studies
Museum Store Association
Association of Partners for Public Lands
Association of Booksellers for Children

At the time of publication, all websites referenced in this document were valid. However, due to the changing nature of the Internet, some addresses may change or the content become less relevant.

It's Your World Books

Africa: A Safari Through Its Amazing Nations!

Australia: The Land Down Under for Mates of All Ages!

Canada: The Maple Leaf Melting Pot Country!

China: A Great Wall Runs Thru It!

Egypt: An Ancient Land of Lore; a Modern Land of Oil and More!

France: The Ooh-La-La Country Everyone Loves!

Germany: The Country of Fairytale Castles and Cutting Edge Science!

Greece: A Volcanic Land of Ancient Olympic Origins!

India: Land of Six Senses and Intriguing Mystery!

Italy: The Country of Amazing Fountains and Awesome Arts!

Japan: An Island Country of Endless Intrigue!

Mexico: A Colorful Land of Exotic Culture!

Middle East: Ancient Countries of Current Events Headlines!

Russia: The Great Bear and Its Dramatic History!

South America: A Continent of Countries of Amazing Proportions!

United Kingdom: The Country of Ships, Sealing Wax, Cabbages, and Kings!

* * * * * * *

Other Carole Marsh Related Titles:

The Mystery of the Ancient Pyramid
Iraq: A Country in Conflict
Afghanistan: A Country at The Crossroads
What Is Islam? Who Are Muslims?

Table of Contents

A Letter from the Author....Page 5
Why Should We Care About the Middle East? ....Page 6
Top Fast Middle East Facts....Page 7
Where in the World Is the Middle East? ....Page 8
In the Beginning ....Page 9
The Amazing History of the Middle East! .... Page 10
Famous Middle Eastern Folks! ....Page 11
Guts and Glory Middle East Style! ....Page 12
Islamic Artists - Faithful to Their Technique! ....Page 13
Arabian Nights - A Flying Carpet Ride to Magical Adventures ....Page 14
The Dead Sea, A Site to See!....Page 15
Take Cover! ....Page 16
Arabic? What's That? ....Page 17
Happy Holidays! ....Page 18
Middle East on the Stage and in the Museums....Page 19
What's for Dinner? .... Page 20
For the Love of Soccer....Page 21
The Wailing Wall...Center of Grief and Joy!.... Page 22
The Middle East Did It First!.... Page 23
The Walled City of Jerusalem - The Writing's on the Wall.... Page 24
The Religion of Islam.... Page 25
War! .... Page 26
Troubled Waters in the Middle East.... Page 27
Modesty Rules! Islamic Fashion.... Page 28
Assorted Architecture!.... Page 29
As They Say in the Middle East... .... Page 30
Further Resources ....Page 31
Answer Key .... Page 32

A Letter from the Author

From the desk of
CAROLE MARSH

Hey kids,

It's your world! It really, really is!
Of course, you already know that, don't you?
You surf the 'net, listen to satellite radio, watch television shows and movies set all around the globe–kids today are much more "worldly" than in the past, and that's a good thing!

Now's a great time to learn something about another part of the world–such as the Middle East. Why? Because one day, you might actually visit there (if you have not already!). You might go to school there–many colleges have ties with international schools around the globe. You might even go on to work in a foreign country!

Many companies have positions in other countries. Companies are "going global" as fast as they can. They have branch offices, manufacturing plants, and customer service centers scattered around the globe!

So, ready or not: YOU are a Citizen of the World! And you'll want to be a good one. How do you do that? You'll find out everything you can about that country, how it's the same, and how it's different from your own country. What language is spoken there? What customs do the people observe? What foods do they enjoy? What do they do for fun? What has happened in this part of the world, and what is happening there now? It's fun ... and the more you learn, the more you will enjoy whatever global opportunity comes your way!

This book is a good place to start your learning journey–so take advantage of the world– IT'S YOUR WORLD, after all ... and guess what? It's a BIG world, after all!

Happy traveling and learning,

Carole Marsh
Always with passport in hand!

Why Should We Care About the Middle East?

How would you like to journey back through time? You can do that in the Middle East, a region with deep-rooted history. The Middle East is the birthplace of Christianity, the home of Judaism, and a sacred place for Islam. The Middle East is also a region of conflict. Differences in religion, culture, and politics cause residents to fight over the land.

The Middle East stretches from Northwest Africa to South Asia over six time zones. It is often called the "crossroads of the world"!

One day you might visit the Middle East and shop in an open Arab market, float in the salty waters of the Dead Sea, or gaze at the Wailing Wall, the most sacred Jewish place in the world. It could happen!

Write home about it!
What will your postcard from the Middle East say?

Top Fast Middle East Facts

Important facts to remember about the Middle East:

- The climate is generally hot and dry.
- The largest supply of oil in the world is in the Middle East.
- Arabic is the most common language.
- The main religion of the Middle East is Islam.
- Saudi Arabia is the only country named after its ruling family.
- The ancient Middle East is sometimes referred to as "The Near East."
- Visitors often travel to the Middle East to see religious landmarks.
- The Middle East is home to Jerusalem, one of the oldest cities in the world.
- Belly dancing is an ancient art form in the Middle East.
- The Dead Sea in Israel is the lowest body of water on Earth.
- The Middle East is the birthplace of Judaism, Christianity, and Islam.

Now, you figure out the rest!

1. The Middle East has the world's largest supply of ___ ___ ___.

2. ___ ___ ___ ___ ___ ___ ___ ___ ___ is one of the oldest cities in the world.

3. Visitors travel to see ___ ___ ___ ___ ___ ___ ___ ___ ___ landmarks.

4. Most people are Muslim, which means they follow the religion of ___ ___ ___ ___ ___.

5. ___ ___ ___ ___ ___ ___ is the most practiced language.

6. The ___ ___ ___ ___ Sea is the lowest body of water on Earth.

The Middle East was named the "Crossroads of the World" because it is the meeting point of three continents, Asia, Africa, and Europe, and because it is a major trading crossroad.

Where in the World Is the Middle East?

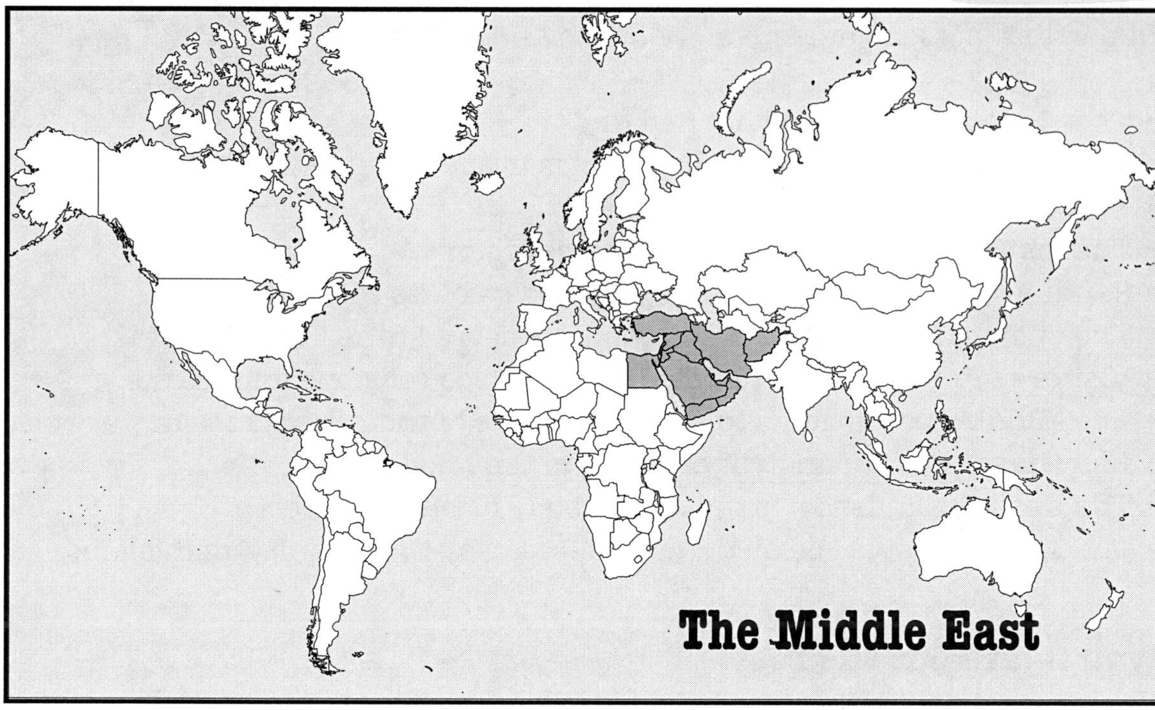

- The Middle East is a cultural region consisting of countries in northern Africa and southwest Asia.
- The Middle East is called the "crossroads of civilization," where cultures, languages, traditions, histories, religions, and economies intersect.
- Maybe you've heard of these Middle Eastern countries in the news: Israel, Jordan, Syria, Saudi Arabia, Egypt, Iran, Iraq, Afghanistan, Kuwait, Oman, Qatar, United Arab Emirates, and Turkey.
- Some important bodies of water are located in the Middle East: the Caspian Sea, the Red Sea, the Mediterranean Sea, the Persian Gulf, the Arabian Sea, the Dead Sea, the Jordan River, the Sea of Galilee, the Tigris River, the Euphrates River, and the Nile River.
- Turkey is the only country in the Middle East located in both Asia and Europe.
- The largest country on the Arabian Peninsula is Saudi Arabia.
- The most abundant natural resource in the Middle East is oil.
- Much of the Middle East has a desert climate—hot and dry. Don't forget to bring your own canteens of water!

Do You Know?

1. The main religion of the Middle East is:
   a. Christianity b. Islam c. Buddhism d. Judaism

2. Which country in the Middle East doesn't have a desert?
   a. Iran b. Lebanon c. Pakistan d. Iraq

In the Beginning...

Much of what we know today comes from ancient Middle Eastern cultures. If it weren't for the Arabs, you couldn't read this page. They invented paper! The counting system used throughout most of the world today probably was developed in India. But the Arabs spread this system to the West, so the numbers it uses are called Arabic. The ancient Egyptians are best known for their amazing pyramids. But did you know they also developed glassmaking? Speaking of developments, Mesopotamia was one of the first civilizations. Talk about being ahead of the game!

The Middle East is the birthplace of monotheism. This means a belief in only one God. Judaism, Islam, and Christianity were born in this region. Jerusalem is a holy city for all three religions. Jews can stand on the ruins of the first Temple, which King Solomon built. The Koran tells Muslims that this is the place where their prophet, Muhammed, rose to heaven. For Christians, this is the place where Jesus was arrested by Roman soldiers. Because Jerusalem means a lot to all three religions, conflicts have arisen among these groups.

Crosswords!

Use your new knowledge to fill in the crossword puzzle.

Across

2. Jerusalem is a holy city for three of these.
3. _________ was one of the first civilizations.
5. The pyramids are an example of this.

Down

1. This is the belief in one god.
4. _________ was invented by the Arabs.

2 E _ _ _ O _ _

3 _ S _ _ _ _ _ _ A

5 _ _ C _ _ _ _ _ _ _ E

The Amazing History of the Middle East!

The Middle East is called the "cradle of civilization." That's because many important "firsts" happened in this area. The Mesopotamians developed the first written language. It had more than 500 letters. Imagine how long it would take to sing your ABCs! Mesopotamians built huge temples and monuments in their cities, and they built reservoirs and canals to store and carry water. They were the first people to use the wheel and they invented the library.

Muhammad

The Middle East is the birthplace of the world's major religions. Judaism and the history of its people were around long before the Babylonian Empire. Muslims know Muhammad as the most perfect prophet, and believe the word of God was revealed to him through an angel to be recorded in the Koran.

Unfortunately, the Middle East is also a center of political, religious, and cultural turmoil. After the Ottoman Empire was conquered during World War I, a struggle resulted between the Arab and Jewish people over the area of Palestine. The Middle East still experiences as much conflict today as it did long ago.

Timeline!

Number these events in the order that they took place, first to last.

__ The Ottoman Empire

__ Mesopotamia

__ World War 1

__ Babylonian Empire

__ Christianity

__ Judaism

__ Struggle for Palestine

__ Islam

Famous Middle Eastern Folks!

Matching!
Match these famous Middle Eastern folks with their accomplishments.

___ 1. As a prophet and central figure of the Islamic faith, I was commanded by God to create the words of a holy book known as the *Qur'an*, or Koran.

___ 2. A renowned scientist and philosopher, I was known as the "prince of physicians." I wrote two famous books, *The Book of Healing* and *The Canon of Medicine*.

___ 3. I once disguised myself as an Arab in order to try and persuade Jordan not to attack Israel. As a Zionist, I was in favor of returning Jewish people to their homeland. I also was the world's third female prime minister.

___ 4. I led the Egyptian Revolution in 1952. I was the second president of Egypt and believed in uniting all Arab nations. I successfully united Egypt with Syria for a short time and called it the "United Arab Republic."

___ 5. I was president of the Palestinian Authority. I promoted a cause called the Palestine Liberation Organization to free Palestine for the Palestinians. I led a peace agreement with the Israeli government in 1993.

___ 6. I took Egypt through the Yom Kippur War of 1973. I worked on a plan to solve the Middle East Crisis, but it cost me my life.

___ 7. My father was prime minister of Pakistan and was hanged by a military government. I resisted military dictatorship and participated in anti-government rallies. I co-chaired the Pakistan People's Party and was the first woman to become prime minister of an Islamic country.

A. Yasser Arafat

B. Anwar al Sadat

C. Muhammad

D. Benazir Bhutto

E. Ibn Sina

F. Colonel Gamal Abdul Nasser

G. Golda Meir

Guts and Glory Middle East Style!

A. The Muslim people needed to appoint a new leader after Muhammad died. His successor would lead the Muslim armies and public prayer.

B. These people lived in the land long before the Arabs. Their language exists only in spoken form. Some consider them backward because they mostly live in rural areas.

C. Muslims disagree on what this practice is supposed to mean. Some say it does not mean "holy war." They call it a struggle to make their lives better or a fight against cruelty.

D. They were Christian prisoners of war organized for the Ottoman army. They were not allowed to grow beards or talk to free men. Despite this, they became powerful in the empire. This threatened the sultan, who had them banished.

E. A Palestinian revolution for independence. The first fight was against Israel when it took control of the West Bank and the Gaza Strip. It became a series of violent attacks and suicide missions in the name of freedom.

Mixed Up!
Match the paragraph to the word that the paragraph describes.

JIHAD ____

CALIPH ____

BERBERS ____

JANISSARIES ____

INTIFADA ____

Islamic Artists—Faithful to Their Technique!

Did you know early Muslims were not allowed to paint human beings or animals? To do so was considered a way of worshiping those objects, and in the Muslim religion it is a sin to worship anything but Allah. Islamic art focuses on flowers, calligraphy, richly patterned shapes, and geometric design.

The followers of Islam used their patterning skills to decorate their books. The most elaborate form is Arabesque, which shows animals and plants in complex patterns. These artists also embellished their buildings by writing verses from the Koran—the Islamic holy book—on tiles. Rugs and cushions were decorated in the same style. Islamic art in fabric is created through intricate weaving patterns.

Arabesque Calligraphy

After the Islamic Empire broke up, each state developed its own art style. In some of these places, the rules against using pictures of people and animals were relaxed. Painters in Iran created mini-paintings of famous people from history.

Draw It!
Get out your crayons. Choose an animal or plant and create an Arabesque pattern using only two colors.

Arabian Nights - A Flying Carpet Ride to Magical Adventures

Could you tell a story if your life depended on it? Princess Scheherazade did—and had to keep it up for 1,001 nights!

King Shahryar planned to marry and execute a new wife each day. But the quick-witted Princess Scheherazade distracted the king by telling him stories. She dragged them out over 1,001 nights to prevent him from killing more innocent girls. Scheherazade charmed Shahryar, but did she save herself from execution?

This is the world of The Thousand and One Nights, a thrilling collection of ancient fables, fairy tales, romances, and historical stories from Arabia, India, and Persia. It's a world where mighty genies conjure up powerful magic, princesses and peasants are BFFs, and daring thieves soar through the night sky on flying carpets! These stories were handed down for several hundred years before they finally were written down. The two best-known adventures from the collection are "The Story of Sinbad" and "The Story of Aladdin's Lamp." What would you do with three wishes? Remember: no wishing for more wishes!

Word Play!

The storytellers who came up with the Arabian Nights used words to express themselves. Now you can, too! Use the letters of Scheherazade's name to create as many words with three letters or more as you can.

Scheherazade

The Dead Sea, A Site to See!

Have you ever heard of the Dead Sea? It is a salt lake between Israel and Jordan. The Jordan River is the only major river that flows into the Dead Sea. The lake is so salty that no animal life can live in it! The lake has no outflow and produces large quantities of raw chemicals. These are exported throughout the world for medicine and industry. People with skin disorders such as psoriasis and arthritis flock to the sea for natural treatment. The Dead Sea is often mentioned in the Bible and is the site of the biblical towns Sodom and Gomorrah.

It is 1,378 feet below sea level and is considered the lowest point on the surface of the Earth on dry land.

It is called the Dead Sea because no plants or animals are able to survive in the water.

It is the world's second saltiest lake in the world after Lake Asal.

Because of the salt content, there is an unusual buoyancy, making it easy for anyone to float in the water.

In recent decades, the Dead Sea has been rapidly decreasing because of the diversion of incoming water.

Create your very own travel pamphlet. Concentrate on an area that interests you. Perhaps you enjoyed learning about the people. Or maybe it was the religions that interested you. Fold a piece of paper into three sections. This will give you six areas on which to put information.

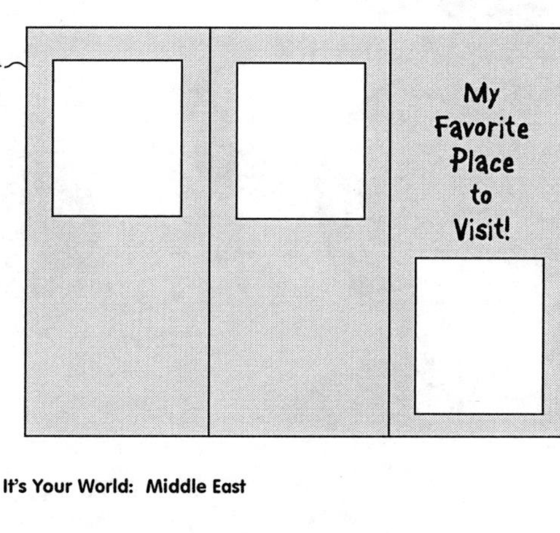

Take Cover!

Customs and culture vary widely from country to country. Sometimes they vary in different regions of the same country. Here are custom and cultural differences observed by people from the Middle East!

- The left hand is considered unclean. Only the right hand can be used to eat, shake hands, or offer a gift.
- In most Middle Eastern countries, women must dress very modestly. Their legs and arms must be covered at all times. In some countries, women are required to wear a scarf that hides their face.
- The Ramadan holiday is celebrated by fasting (not eating) during the day, and feasting from sunset to the early morning.
- Muslims stop whatever they are doing to pray five times a day at exact times.
- Boys and girls are usually not allowed to socialize with each other or to date.
- Marriages are generally arranged by parents or other elders.
- In some areas of the Middle East, food is served from a common plate in the middle of the table. People use their right hand or pita bread to scoop it up.
- Brides are given henna (vegetable dye) tattoos on their hands and feet to ward off bad luck and to bring happiness to the married couple.

Create your own!
As we have seen, customs and cultural activities can help define who we are. Think about your family and friends and come up with some new customs for everyone to try.

Arabic? What's That?

The official language in the Middle East is Arabic. They use a different alphabet. Their alphabet is the Arabic alphabet.

Match it up!
Below are some common Arabic phrases or words. See if you can match them to the English word.

akhdar	salad
ab	red
harr	father
gadaa	no
Adar	March
matihaf	hot
la	museum
Nofember	green
ahmar	lunch
salata	November

Happy Holidays!

Many holidays are celebrated in the Middle East. Each country celebrates an **Independence Day** (sometimes called National Day or Republic Day). Basically, this is the country's birthday. Each country celebrates it on a different day and in a different style.

Many of the Middle East's holidays are religious ones. The three largest religions—Judaism, Christianity, and Islam—were founded in the Middle East. Christians celebrate **Christmas** and **Easter**. The Christmas celebration lasts for 12 days, ending with Epiphany. Christmas Day is celebrated with feasting and gift-giving.

All Jewish holy days begin at dusk the evening before. The Jewish New Year is called **Rosh Hashana** and is celebrated in September. The festival lasts for 10 days and is a time for repentance and self-examination. The 10th day of Rosh Hashana is called **Yom Kippur**. It is known as the **Day of Atonement** and is the holiest day of the year for Jews. It is a solemn day of fasting and praying.

Muslims celebrate **Eid-al-Fitr**, the end of the holy month of Ramadan. During Ramadan, Muslims fast during daylight hours. Eid-al-Fitr is the most important holiday in Egypt and lasts for three days. People feast, exchange gifts, and pray.

Write it down!
Pretend you are visiting the Middle East. Write a letter to your best friend. Tell him or her about the differences between Christmas, Yom Kippur, and Ramadan. What things are the same?

Middle East on the Stage and in the Museums

The Middle East is built on a brilliant arts culture. Its rich heritage of exotic Oriental dance and complex folk music has influenced modern society in the East and West.

2.

Notes

1. The Oud is a basic instrument in Middle Eastern folk music. It is a forerunner to the lute.

2. The correct name for belly dancing is Oriental Dance. The Arabic name is *raqs sharqi*, which means dance of the East.

3. *The Thousand and One Nights* is the only Arabic work that has become popular in the West. Al-Jahshiyari first wrote the stories in Iraq in the 10th century.

4. Calligraphy is a powerful theme in Islamic art. Artist Ali Omar Ermes often focuses on a single letter.

5. The Israel Museum is ranked among the leading art and archaeology museums in the world.

3.

1.

5.

4.

What's for Dinner?

The Middle East has several different cuisines, depending on the country. However, many of these dishes have ingredients in common, such as pita, honey, and sesame seeds. Take a look below at the different foods you could experience in the Middle East.

Baba ghanouj is a dip made from aubergine (what we know as eggplant).

Hummus is a very popular dip that is served with pita bread.

Falafel is made from ground spiced chickpeas, shaped into a ball, and fried.

Khoresh is a Persian word meaning stew. Typically, the main ingredient is the vegetable, not the meat.

RECIPE

Always ask an adult for help when cooking!

Ghoraibi-Butter Cookies

INGREDIENTS

2 cups softened butter
1 cup powdered sugar
1 cup granulated sugar
4 cups all purpose flour
2 cups blanched almond halves
1 teaspoon clear almond extract

MMMMMMMM...this was good!

DIRECTIONS

Preheat oven to 300° F.
Beat butter in a mixing bowl for 5 minutes, or until fluffy.
Stir in almond extract.
Cream in powdered sugar and granulated sugar.
Slowly add in flour. Stir until well blended.
Cover the bowl and chill in the refrigerator for up to 1 hour.
On a floured surface, roll out the chilled dough into a rope that is 1½ - 2 inches thick.
Cut diagonally into diamond shapes and place on ungreased cookie sheets.
Place one almond in the center of each cookie. Bake for 12 minutes.
Carefully remove the cookies from the oven.
Place the cookies on a cooling rack to cool.

For the Love of Soccer

What is your favorite sport? In the Middle East, kids and adults love soccer! There, they call it "football."

Soccer is a relatively simple game. It requires a goal, a ball, and enough room to play! The simplicity of the sport is one of the main reasons why soccer has become so popular throughout the world. England is considered to be the birthplace of soccer as we know it today. Its popularity grew in Middle Eastern nations after World War II.

Many Middle Eastern nations have professional soccer teams that participate in the World Cup and other international tournaments. Governments have built huge soccer stadiums to please enthusiastic fans. For example, the King Fahd International Stadium in Saudi Arabia holds 80,000 spectators! It also has a restaurant that can serve 3,000 people!

Figure it out!
Calculate the answers to these questions about soccer.

1. If a football match is made up of two 45 minute halves with a 15 minute half time, how many minutes will a fan be in the stadium for a match? How many hours?

   ____

2. Your favorite soccer team won 8 out of 12 games this season. What percent of the games did they lose?

   ____

Fast Fact: Egypt's Ahmed "Mido" Hossam is one of the most successful Middle Eastern professional soccer players.

The Wailing Wall... Center of Grief and Joy!

Praying at the Wailing Wall

It's a place of deep emotion. It's a place of amazing history! It's the Wailing Wall in Jerusalem, Israel, the holiest of Jewish sites.

The Wailing Wall is part of the remains of the original temple, which the Romans destroyed in 70 C.E. This is where the Ten Commandments were kept in a golden box called the Ark of the Covenant. The large, open area that faces the Wailing Wall can hold tens of thousands of pilgrims. Each year, thousands of Jewish people visit the Wailing Wall to cry over their many years of suffering.

Visitors to the wall want to touch the stones and feel the holiness that comes from it. Those unable to visit Jerusalem often send in prayers written on paper called tzetzels. They are placed between the 2,000-year-old stones of the wall. The Wailing Wall is a site of national joy where Jewish people come together with their hopes for the future.

Word Fun!

Place the following words in the correct category that describe the past and present of the Wailing Wall.

pilgrimage, Romans, hopes, temple, Ten Commandments, joy, tourists, stones, tzetzels, Ark

Past	Present
______	______
______	______
______	______
______	______
______	______

Middle East Did It First!

Word Fun!

This is fun to do with someone else. Ask a friend for words to substitute for the blanks in the story. Their word substitutions will have a humorous effect when the resulting story is then read aloud.

I want to be the first person to ______________________ (ACTION VERB)

across ______________________ (COUNTRY)! I've been training for this

since ______________________ (MONTH). I'm in ______________________ (ADJECTIVE) shape.

My ______________________ (ADJECTIVE) adventure will begin on

______________________ (FAVORITE HOLIDAY). I won't be hard to miss;

I'll be the one wearing a ______________________ (COLOR)

______________________ (ARTICLE OF CLOTHING) and a pair of matching

______________________ (FOOTWEAR). My faithful friends,

______________________ (FAMOUS ATHLETE) and

______________________ (CARTOON CHARACTER), will be there to cheer for me.

I'm bringing my ______________________ (NOUN) along for good luck.

I'm confident I'll be the first!

Holy Java, Batman!
The drink called coffee was invented in the Middle East.

A Place to Store the Cookies!
The first glass and pottery factory was built in Ar-Raqqah, Syria, in the 8th century.

The Light Goes On!
The first kerosene lamp was invented by Muhammad ibn Zakārya Rāzi in the 9th century.

Soothe That Cough!
The use of syrups for treating coughs comes from medieval Arabic physicians.

Round and Round They Go!
The first windmills were built in Afghanistan, sometime between the 7th and 9th centuries.

Action!
Ovanes Ohanian was the first Iranian film director.

The Walled City of Jerusalem–The Writing's on the Wall

Jerusalem

Jerusalem is called the Walled City. It has been conquered, destroyed, and rebuilt countless times. After 3,000 years of fighting, you'd probably surround yourself with walls, too! Jerusalem's Old City walls have eight gates, but one of them is closed. The closed gate is the Golden Gate (also called the Eastern Gate or the Gate of Mercy). According to Jewish tradition, their king will enter the city though this gate. The gates are angled so you can't enter the city without making a sharp turn. They did this to stop enemies on horseback from charging straight through. Some of the gates have holes through which boiling liquids could be poured on attackers.

Jerusalem is the birthplace of Christianity, the spiritual home of Judaism, and a sacred place for Islam. When King David conquered Jerusalem, he made it the capital of his kingdom. King Herod ruled under the Romans. He was cruel, but he made Jerusalem a beautiful city. After the Babylonians invaded, they banished the Jewish people. The Persians, who defeated the Babylonians, welcomed the Jews back to rebuild the city and its walls.

Today, Jews and Arabs still fight over their claim to the land. Many have tried to bring peace to the city, but so far none have been successful.

Word Fun!

Write five questions that could be asked about Jerusalem.

Example: What makes Jerusalem a holy city?

1. ______________________________?

2. ______________________________?

3. ______________________________?

4. ______________________________?

5. ______________________________?

The Religion of Islam

Mosque

The religion of Islam is more than just a belief. Islam is a complete way of life. The Arabic word "Islam" means submission and obedience. It comes from a word that stands for "peace." People who follow Islam are called Muslims. They believe in only one God, which means Allah in Arabic, whom they believe is The One and Only Eternal God. The heart of the Islamic faith is obedience to Allah's will. Islam is the second most popular religion in the world!

The Prophet Muhammad is the founder of Islam. Muslim beliefs and practices are rooted in the Koran, their sacred book. They believe every word is sacred because Allah revealed them to Muhammad.

Mecca

The place where Muslims pray is called a mosque. When Muslims enter a mosque, they take off their shoes. There is little furniture inside because they pray on mats. There are no pictures or statues either. The walls are decorated with patterns and words from the Koran. Muslims are required to pray five times a day, but Friday is a special day for prayer. Muslims face in the direction of Mecca while praying, because it is the birthplace of Muhammad.

Revealing Answer!

Follow the instructions to reveal the ninth month of the Islamic calendar, and a time when Muslims across the world do not eat during the hours of daylight.

1. Cross off the first and last letters.
2. Cross off any letter "Y."
3. Cross off the letter that represents the Roman numeral 10.
4. Cross off the second "R" from the left.
5. Cross off the fifth letter from the right.
6. Cross off the seventh letter of the alphabet.

Y R Y A X M R A G D L A Y N T

War!

Prime Minister Golda Meir, who resigned following the Yom Kippur War

Conflicts between Israel and Arab states have existed since Israel was created at the end of World War II. They are fighting over a small strip of land! When Israel was formed, it took land from the Arabs, which made them angry. The Israelis believe that they are entitled to the land now known as Israel, while the Palestinians and other Arab states believe that the land is theirs.

In 1973, Egypt and Syria caught Israel off guard when they launched a surprise attack. The Israelis were observing Yom Kippur, their holiest day of the year. The war lasted for a month. Nine other Arab nations joined in the fight, but they couldn't defeat Israel because they didn't work together. The Israelis knew that if they lost, the state of Israel would cease to exist. For Israel, it was a fight to the finish.

The United States supported the Israelis. Because of this, many Arab countries refused to ship oil to the United States. Gasoline prices rose four times higher than before. Gas was in short supply, and many gas stations ran out of gas! Israelis called it the Yom Kippur War. Arabs called it the Ramadan War, because it was fought during their holiest month of the year. The United Nations eventually got both sides to agree to a cease-fire, but there was still no lasting peace.

Cross it off!

Starting with the first letter, cross off every other letter to reveal that Yom Kippur means Day of . . .

S A H T I O F N V E L M Y E R N W T

____

Troubled Waters in the Middle East

For centuries, the countries of the Middle East have fought over oil, religion, and politics. But some world leaders predict that soon the fighting will be over water!

Lack of water in the Middle East threatens all life there—now! Too little rainfall is the main reason there's not enough water. People across the region hope to make up for shortages by reusing wastewater. They also are bringing water to dry areas, creating reservoirs, and removing salt from the ocean water.

Fighting over oil will continue, too. We all depend on oil, and scientists warn that new reserves need to be found. Oil is used to make fuel and gasoline, and to generate electricity. Did you know oil also is used in the clothes you're wearing, medicine, crops, plastic, paints, rugs, CDs, and the ink in your pen? More than half of the Earth's oil lies below the Middle East in underground reservoirs. No wonder people consider oil the most important resource in the region.

Burning oil fields in Kuwait after the first Gulf War

Figure it out!

List the rivers that provide water in the Middle East on the left side, and the seas on the right: Red, Nile, Jordan, Mediterranean, Caspian, Tigris, Dead, Euphrates, Galilee

Rivers	**Seas**
____________	____________
____________	____________
____________	____________
____________	____________
____________	Sea of ____________

Modesty Rules! Islamic Fashion

When you shop, do you snag the hottest fashions to impress your BFFs? Muslim women dress to impress, too. They wear a headscarf called a *hijab* to express their love and respect for Allah. When Muslim women wear the hijab, they are guarding their modesty and showing respect for others by covering up body parts. A Muslim woman in a hijab is making a statement about her identity. Anyone who sees her will know she is Muslim and has a good moral character.

Hijabs come in many different forms. They can be one- or two-piece, long, or square. Muslim women also wear a shawl called the pashmina. The pashmina, made from goat's wool, was made to wear underneath the hijab. Modern pashminas are popular and can be worn with other traditional clothing, as well as with business suits.

Figure it out!

Choose which outfit Christina will wear. Here are some clothes you might see in the Middle East. Color the clothing and draw a line from the piece of clothing to Christina or cut the clothing out and dress her up!

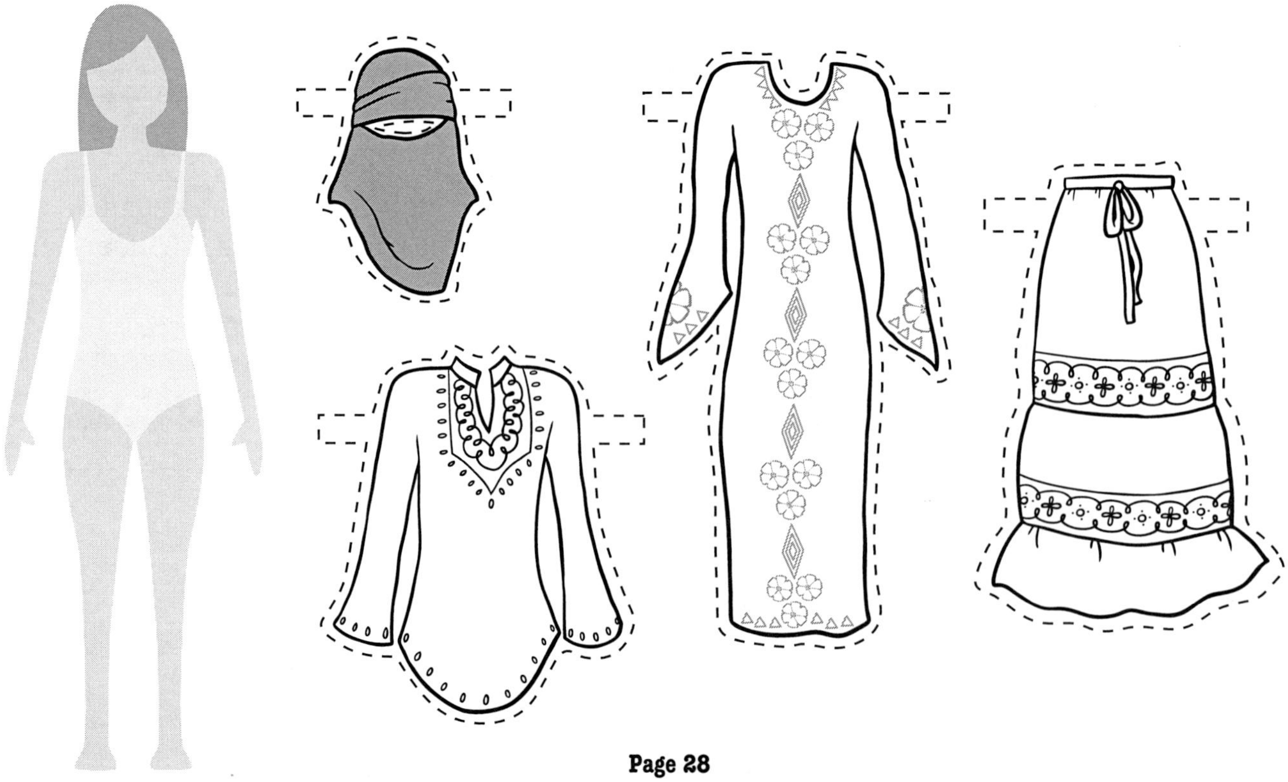

Assorted Architecture!

Figure it out!
Use the following clues to figure out the name of this famous building in Jerusalem.

- It is the most famous Islamic site in the city of Jerusalem.
- The gold crown can be seen from all over Jerusalem.
- It is a shrine—not a mosque—that is famous for its mathematical proportions.
- This landmark was built over a sacred rock, which is the base of the building.
- Built from 691–688 B.C.E., it is the oldest standing Islamic monument today.
- Inside is the oldest Mihrab, or chamber, that points toward Mecca.

2.

4.

6.

1.

3.

5.

As They Say in the Middle East...

Here are a few Middle Eastern words you may already know. Why? Because we use them as "English" words all the time!

algebra: a mathematical term; reunion of broken parts
amen: so be it
ayatollah: miracle of God
balcony: a kind of platform projecting from the wall of a building
beige: a variable color averaging light grayish to yellowish brown
bronze: a metal alloy consisting primarily of copper
caramel: a milky sweet candy
cider: an apple drink
genie: in Arabian folklore, a magical spirit that obeys the person who summons it
harem: the women's quarters; set apart
jar: an earthenware vase
kosher: proper
messiah: anointed
rabbi: my teacher
ream: a quantity of paper, usually 500 sheets
Sabbath: rest
sahib: a friend
sherbet: a frozen dessert made with fruit, syrup, milk, and the white of an egg
syrup: a liquid made of sugar dissolved in water by heating
tabby: a striped cat
tariff: a tax on goods, especially imports and exports
zero: nothing

Further Resources

U.S. Department of State
Bureau of Near Eastern Affairs
http://www.state.gov/p/nea/

Foundation for Middle East Peace
1761 N Street NW
Washington, DC 20036
Phone: (202) 835-3650
Fax: (202) 835-3651
info@fmep.org
http://www.fmep.org/

United Nations
2 United Nations Plaza
New York, NY 10017

The Middle East Center
225 Thomson Hall
Box 353650
University of Washington
Seattle, WA 98195
Phone: (206) 543-4227
Fax: (206) 685-0668
mecuw@u.washington.edu
http://jsis.washington.edu/mideast/

Interesting Websites

http://www.mideastweb.org/

http://www.goisrael.com/Tourism_Eng/Pages/home.aspx

http://www.visitabudhabi.ae/

http://www.saudiembassy.net/

http://www.artdubai.ae/

Answer Key

Page 7
1. oil 2. Jerusalem 3. religious
4. Islam 5. Arabic 6. Dead

Page 8
1. b 2. b

Page 9
1. monotheism 2. religions
3. Mesopotamia 4. Paper
5. architecture

Page 10
6, 1, 7, 3, 4, 2, 8, 5

Page 11
1. C 2.E 3.G 4.F 5.A 6.B 7.D

Page 12
Jihad - C, Caliph - A, Berbers - B,
Janissaries - D, Intifada - E

Page 17

akhdar	green
ab	father
harr	hot
gadaa	lunch
Adar	March
matihaf	museum
la	no
Nofember	November
ahmar	red
salata	salad

Page 21
1. 105 min./1.75 hr.
2. 33%

Page 22

Past	**Present**
Romans	pilgrimage
Ten Commandments	hopes
temple	joy
Ark	tourists
stones	tzetzels

Page 25
Ramadan

Page 26
Atonement

Page 27
Rivers: Nile, Jordan, Tigris, Euphrates
Seas: Red, Mediterranean, Caspian, Dead, Galilee

Page 29
Dome of the Rock